DiSCOVERiNg joE PiLoTES

A Whimsical Exploration of Joe's Inventions

Discovering Joe Pilates

A Whimsical Exploration of Joe's Inventions

Written by Christina Maria Gadar
Illustrated by Taís Haydée Gadar

Gadar, Christina Maria.
Discovering joe pilates: a whimsical exploration of joe's inventions. /Christina Maria Gadar
ISBN-13: 978-0-6928-5151-7
ISBN-10: 0-6928-5151-8

Design Max Kelly
Illustrations Taís Haydée Gadar
Photography Max Kelly
Models Marcelo Gadar, Taís Haydée Gadar, Christina Maria Gadar
Pilates Apparatus Gratz Industries

To order more copies of Discovering Joe Pilates, visit:
www.pilatespersonaltraining.com

For my ray of sunshine and my shining star,
and in loving memory of a special person who helped me see the rainbows again.

Acknowledgments

A big thank you to my creative daughter for the whimsical illustrations that inspired this book, my son and daughter for the beautifully executed Pilates moves captured in the photographs, and Max Kelly for his patience during photo shoots and his expertise in the design and layout of this book.

I also wish to thank:

My husband and my mother for their endless love and support,

My mentors Fernando Bujones and Romana Kryzanowska,

All my teachers, especially Anthony Rabara,

All my children's teachers, especially Julie Burch and Rawley Ryckman,

My students, especially Judith Rock, Michele Glazer, and Ken Deutsch,

My colleagues, especially Suzanne Diffiné,

And the many young children I have had the privilege to teach, especially Benji Gilkey.

"On this machine, you can climb mountains, swim seas, and walk the earth–all while lying down."

-Joe Pilates
Creator of the Pilates System of body-mind-spirit development

Who Was Joe Pilates?

Originally from Germany, Joe Pilates (puh-LAH-teez) moved to New York in 1926. He described his method of exercise as the science of controlling the body, mind, and spirit, and coordinating all three. He called his method Contrology, but today it is known as Pilates. Joe was also a furniture builder who designed the exercise equipment for his method. He wanted children to learn Contrology so that they could develop good habits from the start, instead of having to undo bad habits later on in life. To prove how healthy his exercises made him feel, Joe liked to exercise in the snow wearing only his gym shorts!

There was an inventor named Joe
Who liked to work out in the snow.
He made many things
With barrels and springs
To stretch muscles and help them grow.

The Cadillac

Joe Pilates believed that the bed was the most important piece of furniture in the home. He created many types of beds including the "Automatic Posture Correcting and Rejuvenating Bed" that could be transformed into a gymnasium by attaching springs and bars to the bedposts. This was a very important invention because it allowed students with very weak muscles to exercise while lying down. The current version of this piece of equipment has a cage-like frame above the padded platform so that athletic students can do acrobatic movements on the parallel bars above. Joe's students liked it so much that they named it after the most prestigious car of the time – the Cadillac.

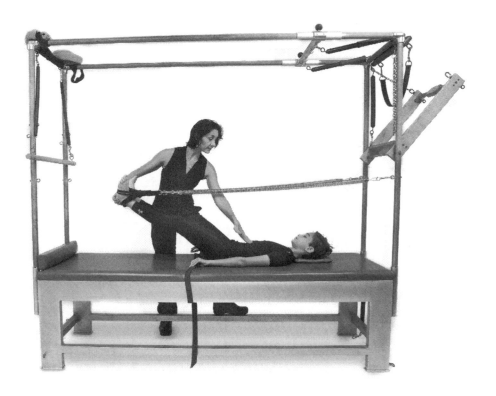

A Cadillac sounds like a car
But this car is slightly bizarre.
It returns you to health
And that is true wealth,
In time you will feel like a star.

The Cadillac Looks Like Monkey Bars

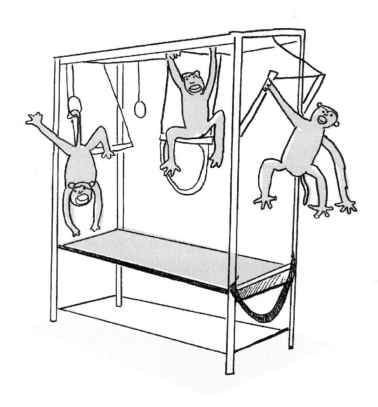

The monkey bars at my new school
Have ravenous monkeys that drool.
These animals feel
That I'd make a nice meal.
Just kidding, today's April Fools'.

Ravenous: extremely hungry

The Reformer

Joe called this famous and versatile invention the Universal Reformer because it improves the body's overall form. He described the Reformer as a "rolling-sled-spring-box machine." The Reformer consists of a board (called the carriage) that slides back and forth on the tracks of a frame. Although the carriage just slides back and forth, students can exercise lying down, sitting, kneeling, standing, and even jumping. Springs attached underneath the carriage provide resistance and serve to lengthen and strengthen the muscles.

Reformers are boards that can glide
Like the skateboards we all love to ride.
The springs will assist
But be sure to resist,
And don't let the carriage collide!

The Reformer Looks Like a Skateboard

A helmet for your skateboard ride
Is a smart choice when you want to glide.
No need to be reckless
Or you'll lose your breakfast,
A bad fall could leave you cross-eyed!

The Wunda Chair

Joe, a former circus performer, invented this chair after watching Chinese acrobats rehearsing on a box. The acrobats would run towards the box and push off it to do flips. He decided that he could improve the box for exercise by adding a step with springs that could be arranged to provide a variety of resistances. He also wanted his students to have a home gym that would help them stay in shape while he vacationed. To make the most use of small New York City apartments, he designed the small exercise box so that it could be flipped over and converted into a comfortable chair when it was not being used for exercise.

Wunda Chair used for exercise.

Wunda Chair converted into a comfortable chair.

Do not be fooled by its small size,
This wonderful chair's in disguise.
Like a Jack-in-the-Box
That shocks when it pops,
There's more to it than meets the eye.

The Wunda Chair Looks Like a Jack-In-The-Box

I once had a good friend named Jack
Who jumped when he sat on a tack.
So, I shrank him right down
And made him a clown,
And put him in Santa's toy sack.

The Arm Chair

At the time Joe developed his exercise method, there were many people with muscle weakness and even paralysis from a disease called polio. He invented a wheelchair with springs that could be used to strengthen the arms or legs. Many of the upper body exercises from his special wheelchair are performed on the Arm Chair today. The Arm Chair is also known as the Baby Chair because it has very thin springs. When stronger students first use the chair they are often surprised to find out that they can get the seatback to move forward with them as they stretch the springs.

This Arm Chair will be a surprise
If you only judge springs by their size.
Both students who are weak
And those at their peak
Are equally re-energized.

8

The Arm Chair Looks Like a Pilot Ejection Seat

A pilot ejection seat flees
A broken plane with lots of ease.
Hit the button and go,
And the next thing you know,
You're flying up high in the breeze.

The Electric Chair

Joe invented a tall chair known today as the Electric Chair or the High Chair. Although none of Joe's equipment uses electricity, the student's energy provides the "electricity" to move the pedal. Joe incorporated everyday objects in many of his inventions. For this chair he added a pair of shovel handles for arm support. Earlier versions of the Electric Chair had arm springs in addition to the spring-based foot pedal (like Joe's rehabilitative wheelchair with springs). The current version uses only the pedal.

Electric Chair may not sound good
But it's just a chair made of wood.
The pedal has spring
And the shovels don't swing,
Its name makes it misunderstood.

The Electric Chair Looks Like a Throne

A throne made of stone looks severe.
So, in case you are king for a year,
A cushion you'll need
For comfort indeed,
Or you'll have a pain in the rear.

The Small Barrel

Joe Pilates worked in beer factories while living in Germany. The wooden kegs used to store beer later became the inspiration for his barrels. The Small Barrel resembles a keg cut in half. It is used to stretch the chest, shoulders, upper back, hips, and legs. Of the three Pilates barrels, it is the smallest, making it perfect for smaller students.

Small Barrels are like root beer kegs,
They're wooden and do not need pegs.
A keg cut in half
With Joe's autograph
Will stretch out your hips and your legs.

The Small Barrel Looks Like a Turtle

There was a sea turtle named Earl
Who happily found a rare pearl.
It fell in the sand
And that was unplanned,
He now has no gift for his girl.

The Spine Corrector

As with the Small Barrel, Joe was inspired by wooden beer kegs when he created the Spine Corrector. It is a medium sized barrel that includes a step. This barrel is named the Spine Corrector because it corrects the alignment of the spine as it stretches and strengthens the muscles. Joe Pilates believed that a healthy spine was one of the most important keys to good health and youthful energy. Joe wrote: "If your spine is inflexibly stiff at 30, you are old; if it is completely flexible at 60, you are young."

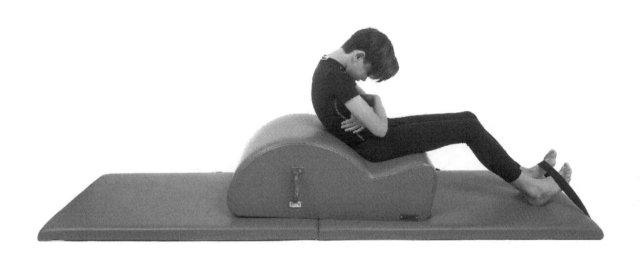

This barrel will stretch out your spine
And hopefully not make you whine.
Resembling a whale
That swims with its tail,
The barrel is simply divine.

Divine: delightful

The Spine Corrector Looks Like a Whale

A blue whale ate four tons of krill
Which gave him a very big thrill.
He got out a map,
Put on a swim cap,
Then swam all the way to Brazil.

The Ladder Barrel

The Ladder Barrel is the largest of the barrels Joe invented. It provides support and stretch while standing, sitting, and even hanging upside down. Joe used to keep his Ladder Barrel near the window of his second floor New York City studio. Keeping the barrel near the window made some students fearful because Joe liked to have them do handstands in between the ladder and the barrel and they worried that their feet would go right through the window!

A ladder and barrel combined
Conceived by a true mastermind.
You lie on the crest
To open your chest,
And then you'll feel truly aligned.

Conceived: to imagine something or come up with a plan
Crest: the top of something

The Ladder Barrel Looks Like a Snail

I had a pet freshwater snail
Who liked to climb on my bed rail.
We'd play hide-and-seek
And I'd never peek,
I just followed his slimy snail trail.

The Twist Pole

The Twist Pole is a long pole that can be used like a ski pole for balance. It can be placed next to the student during an exercise to show him if his body is making the correct shape. And it can be held behind the student's upper back when performing side bends and twists for stretch. There is a well-known photograph of Joe Pilates using the Twist Pole for balance as he stands on his student's stomach! The student in the photograph is a famous opera singer who took regular lessons with Joe in order to strengthen her stomach muscles and increase her breathing capacity. Developing these areas made her a very powerful singer.

The pole by your side makes you feel
As if you are steel, head to heel.
And here's a heads up
For the perfect push-up:
Use your tummy and you'll seal the deal.

The Twist Pole Looks Like a Limbo Bar

What's your most adored party game?
You don't have one? Why that is a shame.
The limbo is mine
Since it stretches my spine,
"How low can you go?" is the aim.

The Push-Up Devices

The Push-up Devices are a miniature version of the parallel bars used in gymnastics. They were designed to increase range in push-ups. The reduced pressure on the wrists, plus the short distance to the floor, make the acrobatic exercises less intimidating. Joe's exercise method was heavily influenced by gymnastics. He developed his ideas at a time when a gymnastic-based strength training movement called Physical Culture was popular in Germany and the United States.

These mini gymnastic bars thrill,
They also require much skill.
You're low to the ground
Where power is found,
No worries if you take a spill.

The Push-Up Devices Look Like Damselflies

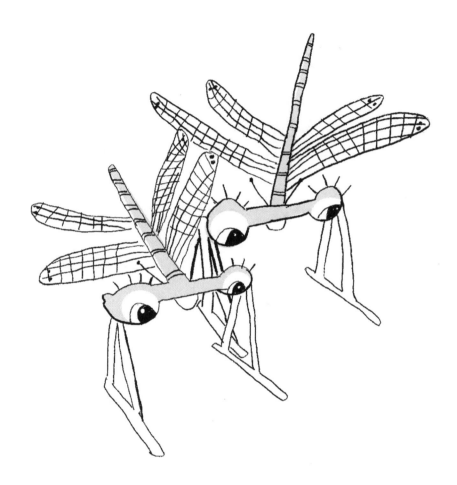

The flight of the blue damselfly
Is a sight to behold in the sky.
With big googly eyes
They're very good spies,
So be sure you do not tell a lie.

The Foot Corrector

Just as a tall building needs a strong foundation to support its multiple stories, Joe Pilates believed that our feet need strength to support our bodies. He invented the Foot Corrector to strengthen the muscles of the feet and correct the posture. The Foot Corrector uses a different type of spring than the springs used on the other pieces of equipment. The springs of the Foot Corrector are called compression springs. They are like the springs used in pogo stick toys. The goal is to compress or push the spring coils down while lifting the body tall.

Most used and abused are your feet,
So why not give them a nice treat?
A good foot massage
Will help camouflage
How tired they feel on concrete.

The Foot Corrector Looks Like a Frog

There once was a tree frog named Stan
Who hid from a crazy old man.
He curled up real tight,
Red eyes out of sight,
Then jumped in his watering can.

The Magic Circle

The idea for the Magic Circle came from the steel hoops of those wooden beer kegs Joe worked with in Germany. Joe added a handle on each side of the ring so it could be placed on the feet, ankles, inner thighs, hands, and even on the head. The most important benefit that comes from proper use of the Magic Circle is better posture. Because the Magic Circle requires students to work harder by using more effort in the right places, some students jokingly refer to the Magic Circle as the "tragic" circle!

A circle that keeps you in shape,
Has more magic than Superman's cape.
When your muscles are long
And your stomach is strong,
Your posture will leave mouths agape.

Agape: wide open with wonder

The Magic Circle Looks Like a Hula Hoop

Irene is a hula hoop queen
Who looks like a twirling string bean.
She moves with a zest
That makes her the best.
Her secret is lots of caffeine.

The Mat

With no outside support from springs, the Matwork requires complete coordination of mind and body. Joe created the other pieces of equipment to help his students get stronger in their Matwork and to make it easier for him to teach. Joe made simple mats for the floor, a Bench Mat that was raised off the floor on four legs, and a special model for doctors' offices called the Divana. The mat on the Divana was fused with the Small Barrel and placed over the Reformer like a lid. Students could work out on the mat and barrel or open the apparatus like a clamshell to reveal the Reformer underneath. When not used for exercise it served as a chaise lounge (a long chair with no arms).

The Mat can be done anywhere.
You just need a small space to spare.
It's the heart and the soul
And the height of control,
Get ready to work, if you dare.

The Mat Looks Like a Flying Carpet

A carpet ride's only a blast
When the sky above's not overcast.
Thunder and lightening
Can be very frightening,
So do check the weather forecast.

Ready to Try a Pilates Move?

Joe Pilates said: "The apparatus isn't necessary; you can do almost as well at home without it – it just makes exercise easier and more fun. Up to eighty years, everyone should be able to touch the floor with both palms without bending the knees. And in order that they may be able to do that, I advise them to start in right now, whether they're six months or sixty years, running around the room on all fours, like an animal, palms flat on the floor, knees unbending."

Don't worry if your knees have to bend or if your palms can't touch the floor right away. It takes practice to walk like an animal the way Joe described it. Just let your head hang like the trunk of an elephant gathering food and pull your bellybutton in towards the ceiling to make it easier to walk your feet forward. Have fun walking on all fours and in time you will be as fit as an animal!

"Exercise is body movement that has a purpose. It is never too early to start."

-Carola S. Trier
Student of Joe Pilates and author of the first Pilates book for children

From Joe to Romana

Romana Kryzanowska became a student of Joe Pilates after injuring her ankle in ballet when she was seventeen years old. As she learned Joe's method of exercise, her ankle healed and soon she was assisting Joe in the studio. After Joe's death Romana kept the Pilates studio running and trained the next generations of Pilates teachers (I was lucky enough to be one of them). Romana inspired her students in many ways. One of the ways she inspired us was by demonstrating the acrobatic moves on the parallel bars of the Cadillac apparatus, and she did this well into her late 80s, almost up to her 90th birthday!

Even though Romana liked to wow us with her demonstrations of super advanced exercises, she taught Pilates with simplicity. She loved to ask aspiring Pilates teachers to define Pilates in three words. At first we struggled to find fancy words, but she taught us that the answer was simple: "Pilates is stretch, strength, and control, and the control part is the most important because that's what makes you use your mind." After spending the day with her in the studio she would always say, "Tell me one thing you learned today. If you learned just one thing today, then I am happy and if you learn one new thing every day, you'll be a genius."

Like Joe, Romana loved to observe the movement of animals and people. After moving from Michigan to Florida as a young girl, she spent her days outside, surrounded by animals (her favorite pet was a goat). As an adult living in New York she loved dining outside at restaurants so she could observe the different ways people walked. She also enjoyed teaching young children ballet and always found a way to incorporate some of the Pilates moves into their dance classes.

Romana came from a family that appreciated all the arts. Her parents loved to paint (her mother painted a portrait of Joe Pilates) and her son became a famous professional ballet dancer. Romana's love of dance, music, art, and poetry influenced the way she taught Pilates. Watching her as she taught was like watching a dance between two people because her movements shadowed the movements of her student. She taught with musicality and loved to tell us to do the exercises with music in our soul as she sang a rhythm to make our movements more dynamic. She believed Pilates was like "poetry in motion" when it was done with a high level of awareness.

Romana spoke Spanish and English fluently and she knew many words in other languages from all her travels teaching Pilates around the world. She loved words so much that she encouraged us to open up the dictionary frequently, pick an unfamiliar word, and use it while teaching. Romana was also fond of picking words that rhymed when she taught. She would say things like, "Take the tension out of your *feet* and put it in your *seat*." She did not want her students to tense the wrong muscles and waste their energy. If she saw a student scrunching up his face while performing a challenging exercise she would say, "Move with big motions, not emotions!" She loved to use very descriptive phrases when she taught because it helped her students move more deliberately. One of my favorite phrases from Romana was, "You need to squeeze the juice out of the exercise; don't just tickle it."

Her laugh was infectious and her sense of humor made learning more enjoyable. If you didn't move with energy, she would jokingly say you were putting her to sleep. She loved to celebrate even if it was not a special occasion. In fact, she would pop open a bottle of champagne in the studio every Friday at noon. Friends and family were important to Romana and her biggest gift as a teacher was that she made all of us feel like part of her family. She didn't just teach us how to do Pilates, she taught us how to enjoy Pilates and she taught us how to enjoy life!

Christina Maria Gadar

Love All Around

Romana would say that the goal
Of Pilates is stretch, strength, control.
She had a devotion
To bodies in motion
And her smile beamed with love from her soul.

Christina Maria Gadar, author

A dual citizen of Brazil and the United States, Christina has spent her entire life working in the art of moving the body efficiently, first as a professional ballet dancer and currently as a Pilates teacher. She has been specializing in private instruction of the original Pilates Method in her Sarasota, Florida studio since 2000. Trained and certified by Joseph Pilates' protégé, Romana Kryzanowska, Christina has a true love for, and devotion to the Pilates Method. She discovered the value of teaching young children Pilates when she began working with a young boy who was diagnosed with leukemia at the age of seven. Since then she has used Pilates to help many children recover from sports injuries, learn about correct body mechanics, and discover the benefits of mindfulness in movement.

Taís Haydée Gadar, illustrator and model (age 8)

Taís Haydée (pronounced "Ta-EESE Eye-DAY") is an exuberant, creative, and talented young girl who loves to draw, write, sew, play outside, and come up with creative inventions. She plays the piano and the trumpet, and takes ballet lessons from her Papa. She loves to turn the Pilates Ladder Barrel into a fort with colorful silks and make obstacle courses in the studio. She has discovered that Pilates improves her awareness about her posture and creates more balance in her body by strengthening the muscles necessary to offset her natural flexibility. Taís does Pilates weekly and her favorite Pilates exercises are the ones that mimic animals. In addition to having her drawings featured in Pilates books, her whimsical Pilates illustrations have been made into greeting cards and another piece of her artwork was chosen to represent her elementary school in their annual fundraiser.

Marcelo Gadar, model (age 10)

Marcelo Gadar is a clever, funny, and athletic young boy who loves to read, toss the football with his friends, and play on his basketball league. He is a very accomplished pianist, a Florida state champion in Brazilian jiu jitsu, and a budding scientist who has most recently extracted the DNA from bananas with the help of his grandmother. Although he had been practicing Pilates before breaking his upper arm, he discovered the value of Pilates after his injury. Sitting out during recess and P.E. class was very frustrating for this athletic boy. As his bone mended, he did Pilates exercises that addressed the healthy parts of his body. During his Pilates lessons he observed how his sadness lightened and his spirits lifted. After his bone healed he did Pilates to regain his flexibility and strength. He now does Pilates weekly as cross-training for his basketball and piano.

Learn More

The quote from Joe Pilates on page ix is from an interview with Beth Brown. It was featured in her article, *How to Stay Fit Lying Down* in the November 1963 issue of <u>Pageant</u> on page 130.

A copy of Joe Pilates' advertisement for the "Automatic Posture Correcting and Rejuvenating Bed" mentioned on page 2 can be seen on pages 148 and 149 in the book, <u>The Joseph H. Pilates Archive Collection</u> (Philadelphia, PA: Trans-Atlantic Publications Inc., July 2000) by Sean Gallagher and Romana Kryzanowska.

The quote on page 4 is from the original pamphlet issued in 1957 by Joseph H. Pilates and Frederick Rand Rogers, <u>The Pilates Pamphlet: Return to Life Through Contrology</u> (New York, NY: American Foundation For Physical Fitness). This pamphlet was reprinted and updated in 2014 by Cathy Strack and Carol J. Craig. The quote is on page 14 in the reprinted version.

The quote from Joe Pilates on page 14 is from his book, <u>Return To Life Through Contrology</u> (Boston: The Christopher Publishing House, published in 1945, reprinted in 1960). It is located on page 12 in the second edition.

The famous photo of Joe mentioned on page 18 can be found on page 97 in the October 8, 1951 issue of <u>LIFE</u>. The name of the article is *Diva With Muscle*.

The vintage Divana apparatus from page 26 was mentioned in the pamphlet, <u>The Pilates Pamphlet: Return to Life Through Contrology</u> by Joseph H. Pilates and Frederick Rand Rogers (details mentioned above). The Divana apparatus that was owned by William Herman (voice coach for clients like Roberta Peters and Lucille Ball) can be seen in the video, <u>Vintage Combo Reformer</u> on www.pilatesanytime.com.

The quote from Joe Pilates on page 28 is from an interview with Marie Beynon Ray. It was featured in her article, *Cutting a Fine Figure* in the August 18, 1934 issue of <u>Collier's: The National Weekly</u> on page 30.

The quote from Carola Strauss Trier on page 29 is from her book, <u>Exercise: What It Is, What It Does</u> (New York, NY: Greenwillow Books, 1982). The quote is taken from page 9 of her book.

Made in the USA
San Bernardino, CA
24 June 2017